7 WAYS TO MAKE MONEY WITH ARTIFICIAL INTELLIGENCE

PRISCILA S. ROSA

2023

HARNESS THE POWER OF ARTIFICIAL INTELLIGENCE TO GENERATE INCOME AND VALUE

Do you want to harness the potential of artificial intelligence to generate income and value in the market? Do you want to discover how to use AI to create innovative solutions, sell high-quality content, teach and learn about any topic, guide and assist other projects or businesses, invest in promising companies, inform, educate, and entertain others, and offer unique products? Then this book is for you!

Imagine exploring the incredible potential of artificial intelligence to boost your income and create additional value in the market. Do you aspire to uncover the secrets of leveraging AI to develop innovative solutions, sell high-quality content, teach and learn about any subject, guide and support other ventures, invest in AI-driven startups and companies, inform, educate, entertain, and offer unique products? If so, then this book is your gateway.

In this book, you will embark on a journey to discover seven compelling ways to monetize artificial intelligence:

1. **Create AI-powered applications:** The first step in your AI income generation journey is to delve into the world of AI-powered applications. Learn how to create cutting-edge apps that harness the power of artificial intelligence to solve real-world problems.

2. **Sell AI-generated content:** Explore the world of AI-generated content and how it can become a lucrative source

of income. Discover how to leverage AI to produce high-quality content that resonates with your audience.

3. **Develop online courses using AI:** Unlock the secrets of designing online courses with AI technology. Learn how to engage and educate your audience while monetizing your expertise.
4. **Offer AI consulting:** Become an AI consultant and guide companies and individuals on their AI journey. Understand the nuances of providing valuable advice in this dynamic field.
5. **Invest in AI companies:** dive into the world of AI investments and explore how you can support and profit from promising AI startups and companies.
6. **Create AI-related content:** Become a thought leader by creating informative and engaging content about artificial intelligence. Learn how to captivate your audience with AI-related insights.
7. **Sell AI products:** Discover how to market and sell products with AI technology. From smart devices to AI-powered solutions, explore the possibilities of this exciting path.

For each of these income-generating methods, you will receive comprehensive explanations, real-life examples, valuable tips, recommendations, and useful resources to put your newfound knowledge into action. You will soon realize that you don't need to be an AI expert to profit from it—just a touch of creativity, curiosity, and a thirst for knowledge.

I wrote this book with the goal of sharing my knowledge and passion for artificial intelligence with you. I hope this book inspires, motivates, and teaches you how to make money in seven different ways with AI. I also hope this book helps you achieve your dreams and goals with AI.

I appreciate your attention and interest in my book. I wish you an enjoyable and enriching read!

CONTENTS

INTRODUCTION

Have you ever wondered how artificial intelligence can become a viable source of income for you? Have you envisioned AI as an ally in creating innovative solutions, offering high-quality content, facilitating the teaching and learning process, guiding and supporting other projects or ventures, investing in promising companies, disseminating relevant information, educating people, entertaining audiences, and enabling the creation of unique products? If your answer to any of these questions is affirmative, then this book is specifically designed for you.

Within the pages of this book, you will have the opportunity to explore seven ways to generate income through artificial intelligence. You will discover how to use AI to profit and add value to the market, fully capitalizing on the opportunities and benefits offered by this technology. It is essential to emphasize that you do not need to be an AI expert to thrive in this context; the key lies in creativity, curiosity, and a willingness to learn.

However, you might be wondering: what exactly is artificial intelligence? Concisely put, we can define it as the ability of machines or systems to perform tasks that would typically require human intelligence, such as image recognition, natural language understanding, decision-making, or problem-solving. AI is causing a revolution in various fields, spanning healthcare, education, entertainment, security, transportation, and many other sectors.

And how can you benefit from this revolutionary movement? Throughout this book, you will be introduced to seven strategies for generating income through AI, which are as follows:

1. **Developing AI-powered applications.**
2. **Selling AI-generated content.**
3. **Creating online courses incorporating AI.**
4. **Offering AI consulting services.**
5. **Investing in companies operating in the field of AI.**
6. **Producing AI-related content.**
7. **Marketing products with AI technology.**

For each of these strategies, you will find detailed explanations, practical examples, valuable tips, sound recommendations, and useful resources that will assist you in putting them into practice. With this book, you will realize that artificial intelligence can be your partner on the journey towards achieving meaningful financial and professional goals.

CHAPTER 1: CREATE APPS WITH AI TECHNOLOGY

Have you ever considered the idea of developing your own app? Have you imagined the potential of millions of users downloading and using your creation? Or perhaps you've fantasized about monetizing your app? If you answered affirmatively to any of these questions, then this chapter is tailored just for you.

In this chapter, you will be introduced to the fascinating world of creating applications powered by AI (Artificial Intelligence) technology. Here, you will discover how AI can become your ally in crafting innovative and practical solutions for real-world problems that affect people. Best of all, you will realize that you don't need to be a professional programmer to create AI-powered apps; all you need is an idea, a tool, and a genuine willingness to learn.

What Is An Ai-Powered App?

An AI-powered app is an application that utilizes artificial intelligence to perform tasks that would typically require human intelligence, such as recognizing images, understanding natural language, making decisions, or solving problems. An AI-powered app can be a mobile app, a web app, or a desktop app.

AI-powered apps offer several benefits, such as:

- ❖ Solving real-world problems for people: An AI-powered app can provide practical and efficient solutions to everyday problems, like communicating in another language, enjoying interactive games, or taking care of one's health and well-being.
- ❖ Offering a unique user experience: An AI-powered app can deliver a personalized and interactive experience to users, adapting content to user profiles, responding to their questions or requests, and suggesting actions or recommendations.
- ❖ Enhancing the design, usability, security, and performance of the app: An AI-powered app can improve various aspects of the application, including design, usability, security, and performance, using techniques like machine learning, natural language processing, or computer vision.

What are the challenges and advantages of creating AI-powered apps?

Creating AI-powered apps can be both challenging and advantageous. Some of the challenges and advantages include:

- ❖ **Challenges**:

  - ➢ **Complexity**: Creating AI-powered apps can be complex because it involves advanced artificial intelligence concepts and techniques like algorithms, models, data, and metrics.

  - ➢ **Security**: Developing AI-powered apps can be risky due to security issues such as privacy, ethics, and data and result reliability.

> ➢ **Competition**: Creating AI-powered apps can be competitive, given the market's strong competition from other AI-powered apps and non-AI apps.

❖ **Advantages**:

> ➢ **Innovation**: Building AI-powered apps can be innovative, allowing you to develop original and differentiated solutions for real people's problems.

> ➢ **Quality**: Creating AI-powered apps can result in high-quality apps, providing a unique and satisfying experience to users.

> ➢ **Profitability**: Developing AI-powered apps can be profitable, as they offer various income-generating avenues, such as ads, in-app purchases, or subscriptions.

How to create AI-powered apps?

To create AI-powered apps, you need to follow some basic steps. These steps include:

1. **Have an idea**: The first step is to have an idea for your app. You need to define the problem you want to solve, your target audience, and the value you want to offer. Ensure that your idea is viable, original, and profitable.
2. **Choose a tool**: The second step is to choose a tool to create your app. You need to select a tool that suits your level of knowledge, the type of app you want to create, and your AI technology needs. You can use AI tools to create AI apps, such as [App Inventor], [Thunkable], or [GPT-3].

3. **Develop your app**: The third step is to develop your app. You need to follow the instructions of the tool you chose and use the AI functionalities it offers. You also need to test and debug your app to ensure it functions correctly.
4. **Publish your app**: The fourth step is to publish your app. You need to choose a platform to distribute your app, such as the Google Play Store, Apple App Store, or Amazon Appstore. Follow the platform's rules and requirements and promote your app.

What are examples of AI-powered apps?

Several examples of AI-powered apps are achieving success in the market. Some of these examples include:

FaceApp: It's an app that uses computer vision to transform people's faces, such as changing their age, gender, style, or facial expression.

Replika: It's an app that uses natural language processing to create a virtual friend that engages in conversations with users on various topics and learns from them.

Duolingo: It's an app that uses machine learning to teach languages, adapting lessons to users' levels and progress.

CHAPTER 2: SELL AI-GENERATED CONTENT

If you're passionate about writing and have a blog, a YouTube channel, an Instagram account, or any other content platform, and the desire to monetize your material is a reality for you, this chapter offers what you need.

Here, you will have the opportunity to learn how to market AI-generated content, exploring various ways to produce material in formats such as text, images, videos, or audio. It's important to note that you don't have to be a professional writer to succeed in selling AI-generated content; all you need is a creative idea, a suitable tool, and a solid monetization strategy.

What Does AI-Generated Content Mean?

AI-generated content is content produced by machines or systems that use artificial intelligence technology to perform tasks that would typically require human intervention, such as writing, illustrating, editing, or narrating. This type of content can be classified into two categories: original content, created entirely from scratch, or derived content, which is based on pre-existing material.

AI-generated content can have several benefits, such as:

❖ Saving time and money: AI-generated content can be produced in large quantities and at high speed, reducing the time and cost of content creation.

❖ Increasing quality and relevance: AI-generated content can be optimized to meet the quality and relevance criteria of the target audience, improving content performance and engagement.

❖ Exploring creativity and innovation: AI-generated content can be inspiring and innovative, generating new ideas and possibilities for content.

What are the challenges and advantages of selling AI-generated content?

Selling AI-generated content can be both challenging and advantageous. Some of the challenges and advantages include:

❖ **Challenges:**

➤ **Originality**: Selling AI-generated content can be difficult because it involves issues of originality, such as plagiarism, copyright, and content authenticity.

➤ **Quality**: Selling AI-generated content can be risky because it involves quality issues, such as coherence, consistency, correctness, and clarity of the content.

➤ **Monetization**: Selling AI-generated content can be competitive, as it involves monetization issues like value, price, demand, and supply of the content.

❖ **Advantages**:

➤ **Diversity**: Selling AI-generated content can be diverse, allowing you to create content in various formats, such as text, images, videos, or audio.

➤ **Personalization**: Selling AI-generated content can be

personalized, as it enables you to adapt content to the profile, interests, and needs of the target audience.

> **Profitability**: Selling AI-generated content can be profitable, as it allows you to generate income through various means, such as ads, sponsored posts, or affiliate programs.

How to sell AI-generated content?

To sell AI-generated content, you need to follow some basic steps. These steps include:

1. **Have an idea**: The first step is to have an idea for your content. You need to define the theme, format, objective, and target audience of your content. Ensure that your idea is viable, original, and profitable.
2. **Choose a tool**: The second step is to choose a tool to create your content. You need to select a tool that is suitable for the type of content you want to create and the AI technology you require. You can use AI tools to create AI-generated content, such as [GPT-3], [DALL-E], or [Lumen5].
3. **Create your content**: The third step is to create your content. You need to follow the instructions of the tool you chose and use the AI functionalities it offers. You also need to review and enhance your content and ensure that it meets the criteria of originality and quality.
4. **Publish your content**: The fourth step is to publish your content. You need to choose a platform to showcase your content, such as a blog, a YouTube channel, an Instagram account, or another content platform. You also need to follow the platform's rules and requirements and promote your content.

What are examples of AI-generated content?

There are several examples of AI-generated content that are being sold or shared on the internet. Some of these examples include:

Texts: These are written content in natural language, such as blog posts, Instagram captions, YouTube scripts, or e-books. An example of AI-generated text is [The Guardian], which published an article written by [GPT-3] on why it is not a threat to humanity.

Images: These are visual content in the form of images, such as illustrations, photos, drawings, or memes. An example of AI-generated image is [This Person Does Not Exist], which creates realistic faces of non-existent people using [StyleGAN].

Videos: These are audiovisual content in the form of videos, such as animations, clips, trailers, or documentaries. An example of AI-generated video is [Synthesia], which creates customized videos using voice and image synthesis.

Audios: These are audio content in the form of audio, such as music, podcasts, narrations, or sound effects. An example of AI-generated audio is [Jukebox], which creates original songs or imitates music styles using the WaveNet neural network.

CHAPTER 3: CREATE ONLINE COURSES USING AI

If you have a passion for teaching and want to share your knowledge or skills with others, with the intention of monetizing your expertise, then this chapter is for you.

Here, you will explore how to create online courses using AI (Artificial Intelligence) technology. You will discover how AI can be a powerful ally in crafting courses on any subject in which you are proficient. It's important to emphasize that you don't need to be a professional teacher to create online courses with the assistance of AI; what matters is having the content, using the right tools, and having an appropriate online teaching platform.

What Constitutes an Online Course Using AI Technology?

An online course using AI technology is a course designed by machines or systems that make use of artificial intelligence to perform functions that would typically be attributed to human intelligence. This includes tasks such as course planning, structuring, presentation, and assessment. It's worth mentioning that an online course using AI technology can be conducted synchronously, happening in real-time, or asynchronously, with pre-recorded content available for later access.

An online course using AI can have several benefits, such as:

- ❖ Teaching and learning about any subject: An online course using AI can cover any topic you master or want to learn, such as languages, programming, business, or hobbies.
- ❖ Adapting content to each student: An online course using AI can personalize the course content based on each student's level, pace, and learning style, enhancing retention and satisfaction.
- ❖ Offering an interactive and dynamic experience: An online course using AI can provide an interactive and dynamic experience for students, allowing them to ask questions, provide feedback, suggest activities, or recommend resources.

What are the challenges and advantages of creating online courses using AI?

Creating online courses using AI can present both challenges and advantages. Some of the challenges and advantages include:

- ❖ **Challenges**:

  - ➤ **Quality**: Creating online courses using AI can be challenging because it involves quality issues, such as coherence, consistency, correctness, and clarity of course content.

  - ➤ **Security**: Creating online courses using AI can be risky, as it involves security issues such as privacy, ethics, and the reliability of course data and results.

  - ➤ **Competition**: Creating online courses using AI can be competitive, as it involves significant competition in the market, both from other online courses using AI and from traditional online courses.

- ❖ **Advantages**:

  - ➢ **Cost-Efficiency**: Creating online courses using AI can be cost-efficient, as it allows you to reduce the time and cost of course creation.

  - ➢ **Scalability**: Creating online courses using AI can be scalable, as it enables you to reach a large number of students in different locations and time zones.

  - ➢ **Profitability**: Creating online courses using AI can be profitable, as it allows you to generate income through various means, such as direct sales, subscriptions, or advertisements.

How to create online courses using AI?

To create online courses using AI, you need to follow some basic steps. These steps include:

1. **Have content**: The first step is to have content for your course. You need to define the theme, objective, target audience, and value of your course. You also need to ensure that your content is viable, original, and profitable.
2. **Choose a tool**: The second step is to choose a tool to create your course. You need to select a tool that is suitable for the type of course you want to create and the AI technology you require. You can use AI tools to create AI-powered courses, such as [OpenAI Codex], [Teachable Machine], or [Udemy AI].
3. **Create your course**: The third step is to create your

course. You need to follow the instructions of the tool you chose and use the AI functionalities it offers. You also need to review and enhance your course and ensure that it meets the criteria of quality and relevance.

4. **Publish your course**: The fourth step is to publish your course. You need to choose a platform to distribute your course, such as Udemy, Coursera, or Skillshare. You also need to follow the platform's rules and requirements and promote your course.

What are examples of online courses using AI?

There are several examples of online courses using AI that are being offered or consumed on the internet. Some of these examples include:

Language Courses: These are courses that use AI to teach languages, adapting lessons to the level and progress of students, such as [Duolingo], [Rosetta Stone], or [Babbel].

Programming Courses: These are courses that use AI to teach programming, generating code, examples, and exercises for students, such as [Codecademy], [DataCamp], or [Code.org].

Business Courses: These are courses that use AI to teach business, analyzing data, trends, and success cases for students, such as [Harvard Business School Online], [Udacity], or [edX].

CHAPTER 4: OFFER AI CONSULTING SERVICES

Do you have experience in artificial intelligence? Do you know how to apply or integrate AI into projects or businesses? Do you want to turn your AI knowledge into a source of income? If you answered yes to any of these questions, this chapter is tailored to your needs.

In this section, you will be guided on how to offer AI consulting services. You will discover how artificial intelligence can be your powerful ally in assisting companies or individuals who need guidance or support in implementing AI into their ventures. It's important to note that you don't need to be a renowned AI expert to become an AI consultant; what matters is having the skill, the right tools, and an effective marketing strategy.

So, what exactly does AI consulting entail?

AI consulting involves providing guidance, assistance, or solutions to companies or individuals seeking support in using or integrating artificial intelligence into their projects or businesses. This service can be conducted both in-person and online, through meetings, calls, emails, or digital platforms, adapting to the clients' needs.

AI consulting can have several benefits, such as:

❖   Solving real client problems: AI consulting can offer practical and efficient solutions to problems that clients face in their daily operations, such as improving digital marketing, analyzing data, or developing websites.

❖   Increasing credibility and authority: AI consulting can enhance the credibility and authority of the consultant, demonstrating their knowledge and experience in artificial intelligence.

❖   Generating income and value: AI consulting can generate income and value for the consultant, as it allows them to charge by the hour or per project, depending on the complexity and scope of the work.

What are the challenges and advantages of offering AI consulting?

Offering AI consulting services can present both challenges and advantages. Some of the challenges and advantages include:

❖ **Challenges**:

➢   **Demand**: Offering AI consulting can be challenging because it involves issues of demand, such as finding clients, understanding their needs and expectations, and satisfying them.

➢   **Expertise**: Offering AI consulting can be risky, as it involves issues of expertise, such as staying updated on AI innovations, trends, and best practices.

➢   **Competition**: Offering AI consulting can be competitive, as it involves significant competition in the market, both from other AI consultants and from professionals without AI expertise.

- ❖ **Advantages**:

  - ➤ **Flexibility**: Offering AI consulting can be flexible, as it allows you to work at different times, places, and on various projects, depending on your availability and preference.

  - ➤ **Learning**: Offering AI consulting can be a learning experience, as it allows you to acquire new knowledge and skills in artificial intelligence while dealing with different challenges and situations.

  - ➤ **Recognition**: Offering AI consulting can be a recognition, as it enables you to build a reputation and a network of contacts in the market by delivering satisfactory results and receiving recommendations from clients.

How to offer AI consulting?

To offer AI consulting, you need to follow some basic steps. These steps include:

1. **Have a skill**: The first step is to have a skill in artificial intelligence. You need to define your area of expertise, your level of knowledge, and your unique selling proposition. You also need to ensure that your skill is viable, original, and profitable.
2. **Choose a tool**: The second step is to choose a tool to offer your consulting services. You need to select a tool that is suitable for the type of consulting you want to provide and the AI technology you require. You can use AI tools to offer consulting with AI, such as [Google Cloud AI], [IBM Watson], or [Microsoft Azure AI].

3. **Develop your work**: The third step is to develop your work. You need to follow the tool's instructions and use the AI features it offers. You also need to follow the client's specifications and ensure that your work meets the criteria of quality and relevance.
4. **Deliver your work**: The fourth step is to deliver your work. You need to choose a method of delivering your work, such as a report, a presentation, or a demonstration. You also need to adhere to deadlines and agreements with the client and receive your payment.

What are examples of AI consulting?

There are several examples of AI consulting that are being provided or hired on the internet. Some of these examples include:

Digital Marketing Consulting: This is consulting that uses AI to help clients improve their digital marketing efforts, such as optimizing SEO, creating ads, generating leads, or increasing sales.

Data Analysis Consulting: This is consulting that uses AI to help clients analyze data, such as extracting insights, making predictions, making decisions, or solving problems.

Web Development Consulting: This is consulting that uses AI to help clients develop websites, such as creating layouts, generating content, testing features, or improving performance.

CHAPTER 5: INVEST IN AI COMPANIES

Are you interested in making investments? Do you want to be part of the artificial intelligence revolution and reap the rewards of the growth and profitability of companies operating in this sector? If you answered yes to any of these questions, this chapter is tailored for you.

In this section, you will be instructed on how to invest in AI companies. You will discover how artificial intelligence can assist you in identifying and investing capital in companies with potential for expansion and profitability. It's important to note that you don't need to be a professional investor to allocate resources to AI companies; what matters is having the appropriate capital, using the right tools, and establishing a solid investment strategy.

So, what exactly does it mean to invest in AI companies?

Investing in AI companies involves allocating financial resources to organizations that use or develop artificial intelligence in their products, services, or processes. This type of investment can be made through various vehicles, such as stocks, investment funds, cryptocurrencies, or other AI-related assets, providing multiple options for investors.

Investing in AI companies can have several benefits, including:

- ❖ Generating profit and value: Investing in AI companies can yield profit and value for the investor by allowing them to participate in the financial results and growth of AI companies.
- ❖ Diversifying the portfolio: Investing in AI companies can diversify the investor's portfolio by providing exposure to different sectors, markets, and risks related to AI.
- ❖ Encouraging innovation: Investing in AI companies can encourage innovation by supporting and funding companies that are creating original and differentiated solutions to real-world problems.

What are the challenges and advantages of investing in AI companies?

Investing in AI companies can be both a challenge and an advantage. Some of the challenges and advantages include:

- ❖ **Challenges**:

  - ➢ **Risk**: Investing in AI companies can be risky, as it involves issues of volatility, uncertainty, regulation, and market competition in the AI industry.

  - ➢ **Return**: Investing in AI companies can be time-consuming, as it involves issues related to the maturity, scalability, profitability, and sustainability of AI companies.

  - ➢ **Information**: Investing in AI companies can be complex, as it involves issues of data quality, quantity, accessibility, and reliability, as well as the need for accurate information for making investment decisions.

❖ **Advantages**:

> **Potential**: Investing in AI companies can be promising, as it allows you to tap into the potential of artificial intelligence, one of the most revolutionary and lucrative technologies of our time.

> **Opportunity**: Investing in AI companies can be timely, as it allows you to anticipate market trends and demands in the ever-evolving and expanding AI market.

> **Participation**: Investing in AI companies can be rewarding, as it allows you to be a part of the history and future of artificial intelligence, which is transforming the world in various fields.

How to invest in AI companies?

To invest in AI companies, you need to follow some basic steps. These steps include:

1. **Have capital**: The first step is to have capital for investment. You need to determine the amount you want or can invest in AI companies. You also need to ensure that your capital is sufficient, suitable, and safe for investing in AI companies.
2. **Choose a tool**: The second step is to choose a tool for investment. You need to select a tool that is suitable for the type of investment you want to make and the AI technology you require. You can use AI tools for AI-assisted investments, such as [Robinhood], [Wealthfront], or [NapoleonX].
3. **Invest in AI companies**: The third step is to invest in AI companies. You need to follow the instructions of the

tool you have chosen and use the AI features it offers.You also need to follow the analyses, forecasts, decisions, and recommendations of the tool and ensure that your investment meets the criteria of risk and return.

4. **Monitor your investment**: The fourth step is to monitor your investment. You need to track the performance, value, and results of your investment in AI companies. You also need to adjust, maintain, or exit your investment according to your strategy and goal.

What are examples of AI companies?

There are several examples of AI companies that are being invested in or financed on the internet. Some of these examples include:

Startups: These are early-stage companies that use or develop artificial intelligence in their products, services, or processes, aiming to innovate and grow in the market. An example of an AI startup is [OpenAI], which creates and researches general artificial intelligence with the goal of creating beneficial AI for humanity.

Tech Giants: These are established companies that use or develop artificial intelligence in their products, services, or processes, aiming to lead and dominate the market. An example of a tech giant in AI is [Google], which conducts AI research and development in various areas such as search, advertising, virtual assistants, translation, healthcare, and education.

Specialized Funds: These are investment funds dedicated to investing in companies that use or develop artificial intelligence in their products, services, or processes, with the goal of generating profit and value for investors. An example of a fund specializing in AI is the [AI Fund], which invests in companies creating AI solutions for real-world problems.

CHAPTER 6: CREATE CONTENT ABOUT AI

If you're passionate about artificial intelligence, want to share your knowledge and opinions on the subject, and are interested in monetizing your AI-related content, this guide has been specially developed to meet your needs.

In this context, you will receive guidance on how to create AI-related content. You will discover how AI can be your ally in producing material in various formats, such as blogs, podcasts, videos, or books. It's important to note that you don't need to be an AI expert to create content on the topic; all you need is experience, the right tools, and an appropriate platform for dissemination.

So, what is AI-related content?

AI-related content is content that addresses the topic of artificial intelligence, whether through information, education, or entertainment. AI-related content can have various objectives, such as:

- ❖ Inform: AI-related content can inform people about the latest news, trends, and curiosities in artificial intelligence, such as news articles or infographics.
- ❖ Educate: AI-related content can educate people about the concepts, techniques, and applications of artificial

intelligence, such as tutorials, courses, or webinars.

❖ Entertain: AI-related content can entertain people with stories, games, or humor related to artificial intelligence, such as fiction, adventure, or comedy.

AI-related content can have several benefits, including:

❖ Increasing knowledge and awareness: AI-related content can increase people's knowledge and awareness of artificial intelligence, its benefits, and its challenges.

❖ Generating engagement and influence: AI-related content can generate engagement and influence people on the topic of artificial intelligence, their opinions, and actions.

❖ Creating value and income: AI-related content can create value and income for the content creator through recognition, reputation, and monetization.

What are the challenges and advantages of creating AI-related content?

Creating AI-related content can be both a challenge and an advantage. Some of the challenges and advantages include:

❖ **Challenges**:

➢ **Research**: Creating AI-related content can be difficult, as it involves research issues such as the quality, quantity, accessibility, and reliability of sources and data about artificial intelligence.

➢ **Authority**: Creating AI-related content can be risky, as it involves issues of authority, including credibility, experience, ethics, and responsibility of the content creator regarding artificial intelligence.

➢ **Monetization**: Creating AI-related content can be

competitive, as it involves monetization issues such as value, price, demand, and supply of content related to artificial intelligence.

❖ **Advantages**:

➢ **Diversity**: Creating AI-related content can be diverse, as it allows you to create content in various formats, such as blogs, podcasts, videos, or books.

➢ **Personalization**: Creating AI-related content can be personalized, as it allows you to tailor the content to the profile, interests, and needs of the target audience.

➢ **Profit**: Creating AI-related content can be profitable, as it enables you to generate income through various means, such as advertisements, sponsored posts, or affiliate programs.

How to create AI-related content?

To create AI-related content, you need to follow some basic steps. These steps include:

1. **Have experience**: The first step is to have experience in artificial intelligence. You need to determine your area of expertise, your level of knowledge, and your unique perspective. You also need to verify if your experience is viable, original, and potentially profitable.
2. **Choose a tool**: The second step is to choose a tool for creating your content. You need to select a tool that is suitable for the type of content you want to create and the AI technology you require. You can use AI tools to create content with AI, such as [GPT-3], [DALL-E], or [Lumen5].
3. **Create your content**: The third step is to create your

content. You need to follow the instructions of the tool you have chosen and use the AI features it offers. You also need to review and enhance your content to ensure that it meets quality and relevance criteria.

4. **Publish your content**: The fourth step is to publish your content. You need to choose a platform to disseminate your content, such as a blog, a YouTube channel, an Instagram account, or another content platform. You also need to follow the rules and requirements of the platform and promote your content.

What are examples of AI-related content?

There are several examples of AI-related content being created or consumed on the internet. Some of these examples include:

Blogs: These are written content pieces that address the topic of artificial intelligence through information, education, or entertainment. An example of an AI blog is [Machine Learning Mastery], which teaches machine learning concepts and techniques to beginners and professionals.

Podcasts: These are audio content pieces that cover the topic of artificial intelligence through information, education, or entertainment. An example of an AI podcast is the [AI Podcast], which interviews experts and personalities about the latest developments and curiosities in artificial intelligence.

Videos: These are audiovisual content pieces presented in video format that address the topic of artificial intelligence through information, education, or entertainment. An example of an AI video is [Two Minute Papers], which summarizes key scientific papers on artificial intelligence in two minutes.

Books: These are written content pieces in natural language that address the topic of artificial intelligence through information, education, or entertainment. An example of an AI book is [Life 3.0], which explores the implications and challenges of artificial intelligence for humanity.

CHAPTER 7: SELL AI PRODUCTS

If you have an affinity for creating products and aspire to turn an idea or skill into a profitable product, especially one related to artificial intelligence, then this chapter will prove valuable to you.

In this section, you will receive guidance on how to market AI products. You will discover how AI can be a powerful ally in designing products that incorporate artificial intelligence in their features, functionalities, or benefits.

It's important to note that you don't need to be an engineer or designer to sell AI products; what's essential is having an innovative product, using the right tools, and implementing an effective sales strategy.

So, what defines an AI product?

An AI product is one that utilizes or integrates artificial intelligence into its features, functionalities, or advantages. These products can come in physical formats, such as robots, drones, or toys, as well as digital formats, such as applications, games, or e-books, offering a wide variety of possibilities for entrepreneurs and creators.

An AI product can have several benefits, including:

❖ Solving real-world problems for people: An AI product can offer practical and efficient solutions to problems people face in their daily lives, such as organizing, having fun, or taking care of themselves.

❖ Providing a unique user experience: An AI product can provide a personalized and interactive experience for users, such as adapting the product to the user's profile, responding to their questions or requests, or suggesting actions or recommendations.

❖ Improving the design, usability, security, and performance of the product: An AI product can enhance various aspects of the product, including design, usability, security, and performance, using techniques like machine learning, natural language processing, or computer vision.

What are the challenges and advantages of selling AI products?

Selling AI products can be both challenging and advantageous. Some of the challenges and advantages include:

❖ **Challenges**:

> **Development**: Selling AI products can be challenging as it involves development issues such as complexity, cost, and time required to create AI products.

> **Security**: Selling AI products can be risky as it involves security issues such as privacy, ethics, and the reliability of data and results from AI products.

> **Competition**: Selling AI products can be competitive as there is significant competition in the market, both from other AI products and from products without AI technology.

❖ **Advantages**:

> **Innovation**: Selling AI products can be innovative as it allows you to develop original and differentiated products that use or incorporate artificial intelligence in their features, functions, or benefits.

> **Quality**: Selling AI products can be of high quality as it enables you to offer products that meet the needs and expectations of users.

> **Profit**: Selling AI products can be profitable as it allows you to generate income through various means, such as direct sales, subscriptions, or advertising.

How to sell AI products?

To sell AI products, you need to follow some basic steps. These steps include:

1. **Have a product**: The first step is to have a product to sell. You need to define what your product is, what it's AI feature, function, or benefit is, and what its value is. You also need to verify if your product is viable, original, and potentially profitable.
2. **Choose a tool**: The second step is to choose a tool to create your product. You need to select a tool that is suitable for the type of product you want to create and the AI technology you require. You can use AI tools to create products with AI, such as [Arduino], [Raspberry Pi], or [TensorFlow].
3. **Create your product**: The third step is to create your product. You need to follow the instructions of the tool you have chosen and use the AI features it offers. You also need to test and debug your product to ensure that

it functions correctly.

4. **Sell your product**: The fourth step is to sell your product. You need to choose a way to sell your product, such as a website, an online store, or a fair. You also need to follow the rules and requirements of the sales method and promote your product.

What are examples of AI products?

There are several examples of AI products being sold or purchased on the internet. Some of these examples include:

Robots: These are physical products that use AI to perform tasks that would typically require human intelligence, such as cleaning, cooking, or playing. An example of an AI robot is [Roomba], which uses computer vision to autonomously and intelligently vacuum floors.

Drones: These are physical products that use AI to fly and capture images or videos autonomously and intelligently. An example of an AI drone is [Skydio], which uses computer vision to avoid obstacles and follow people or objects.

Toys: These are physical products that use AI to entertain and educate children interactively and intelligently. An example of an AI toy is [Cozmo], which uses natural language processing and machine learning to recognize, speak, and learn with children.

CONCLUSION

You've reached the end of this book, and I hope you've enjoyed it and learned a lot from it. My goal was to show you 7 ways to make money with artificial intelligence, one of the most revolutionary and lucrative technologies of our time.

You've seen how AI can enable you to create applications, sell content, develop online courses, offer consultancy, invest in AI companies, create content, and sell products with AI technology. You've also received practical guidance and resources to implement each of these methods.

Now, it's your turn to put into practice what you've learned in this book. Don't be afraid to experiment, test, and learn with AI. You don't need to be an AI expert to make money with it; all you need is creativity, curiosity, and a willingness to learn. Seize the opportunities and benefits that AI offers to generate income and value in the market.

Artificial intelligence provides numerous profit opportunities. Find your place in this rapidly expanding market and take advantage of all the benefits that AI can bring to your business.

Thank you very much, and until next time!

If you enjoyed this book, please leave a positive review on Amazon. This will help me reach more readers and continue writing about artificial intelligence. I would be very grateful for your support.

GLOSSARY

In this glossary, you will find definitions for some of the technical terms used in this book. The terms are listed in alphabetical order.

Algorithm: It is a sequence of steps or rules that defines how to solve a problem or perform a task.

Computer Vision: It is a branch of artificial intelligence that focuses on how machines can see, recognize, and interpret images or videos.

Data: It is information or facts that can be used to feed, train, or test an AI algorithm or model.

Machine Learning: It is a branch of artificial intelligence that studies how machines can learn from data and experiences without being explicitly programmed for it.

Metric: It is a measure or indicator that can be used to evaluate the performance or quality of an AI algorithm or model.

Model: It is a mathematical or computational representation of a phenomenon or system that can be used for predictions or simulations.

Natural Language Processing: It is a branch of artificial intelligence that deals with how machines can understand, generate, and manipulate natural language, such as text or speech.